MORE
WEIRD MOMENTS
IN SPORTS
BY BRUCE WEBER

DESIGNED AND ILLUSTRATED
BY HOWIE KATZ

SCHOLASTIC INC.
New York Toronto London Auckland Sydney

In memory of my father,
Paul Weber, who would have
enjoyed this.

ISBN 0-590-43522-1

12 11 10 9 8 7 6   4/9

Printed in the U.S.A.   01

CONTENTS

IN THE BIG-INNING

FOREWORD

A lot of people take sports too seriously. A former football coach is writing a book about football and war. Writers and fans ask players about their views on world affairs. And some TV announcers describe the action on the field as if it were a religious ceremony.

Wrong. Wrong. And wrong. Even though some people do take sports too seriously, sports are still basically kids' games grown up. And just because the players are paid incredible sums for sometimes so-so play doesn't mean the basic ideas have changed.

One writer calls sports "the world of fun and games." Another refers to it as "the toy department." That's more like it. Sports— from Little League to high school to college to the pros—are meant to be fun. For everyone.

That's what *More Weird Moments in Sports* is all about. Whether your game is baseball, football, or basketball, you'll find plenty of wacky hits and errors to fracture your funny bone. And we've got a whole section of bloopers in hockey, soccer, golf, track, and racing that you can share with your friends.

So lace up your sneakers—or kick off your shoes—and settle back with those weird moments that most players and coaches would like to forget. Then you'll know why sports should be "the world of fun and games."

DIAMOND
DOOSIES

THWACK

THE PHANTOM PICK-OFF

University of Miami baseball coach Ron Fraser called it "The Grand Illusion." Wichita State called it lousy. And the fans in Omaha's Rosenblatt Stadium called it the most amazing play they'd ever seen.

As Miami moved toward the 1982 College World Series championship, the road was blocked by speedy Wichita State. The Shockers had stolen 300 bases in their first 83 games. And lightning-quick Phil Stephenson had pilfered 86 bags in 90 tries.

Fraser and his assistants conceived "The Grand Illusion" and had their players rehearse it. "We never knew if we'd have a chance to use it," said Fraser. "The situation had to be right."

In the sixth inning of the Miami-Wichita game, the situation was perfect. The sun was just about ready to set over the left-field corner. Its rays shone brightly in the eyes of the Wichita first-base coach and the runner, Phil Stephenson.

Miami pitcher Mike Kasprzak threw over

to first a couple of times to keep Stephenson close. Then he delivered a pitch to the plate. Now was time for "The Grand Illusion."

Kasprzak carefully slipped his back foot off the mound. He didn't want a balk to spoil the play. Then he *pretended* to throw the ball over to first.

The runner, Stephenson, dove back into the bag. The Miami first baseman sprawled across the runner as if trying to corral a wild throw.

The Miami second baseman began shouting, "Ball! Ball!" as he pointed toward the right-field corner. Every player in the Miami dugout moved to the top step and yelled, "Ball! Ball!" Even the catcher in the Miami bullpen down the right-field line began shouting, "Ball! Ball!"

The Miami first baseman chased the imaginary ball down the line. He was followed closely by the first-base umpire, who was also fooled.

The Academy Award performance totally tricked Stephenson. He picked himself up and lit out for second base. Pitcher Kasprzak allowed Stephenson to get up a good head of steam, then calmly tossed the ball to his shortstop. Stephenson was out by a mile.

A big play? Could be. Miami hung on to win the game 4–3. The Hurricanes then went on to win the championship.

NIGHT AND DAY

When the San Francisco Giants and Philadelphia Phillies got together for a Wednesday night game in Philly early in 1981, they expected to spend nine innings and about three hours together.

They played the nine innings, but their visit took them one-eighth of the way into Thursday.

It took a two-run homer by the Giants' Jack Clark in the top of the eighth to win the game. By that time only 200 fans were still around.

Rain had caused a pair of delays totaling five hours, and the final pitch wasn't delivered until 3:12 A.M., nearly eight hours after the 7:35 P.M. start.

HOME RUN THE SECOND

John Franklin Baker was better known as "Home Run" Baker. The name didn't really fit. In his best season, 1913, he swatted only 12 homers.

But another Baker—Floyd—made "Home Run" look absolutely fabulous.

Floyd, an infielder who shuttled between six American League clubs in the early 1950s, came to bat 2,280 times during his major league career. His home-run total: *one*.

LONG DAY'S JOURNEY

You've probably never heard of Harley "Doc" Parker, but he occupies a special spot in the all-time baseball record book. Parker toiled for the Chicago Cubs and Cincinnati Reds for nine seasons during baseball's early years (1893–1901). But one outing in 1901 made "Doc" think about another career.

Parker went the full nine innings on that fateful day, allowing "only" 21 runs and 26 hits. Unfortunately, relief pitching hadn't really been invented yet.

PHANTOM OF THE BALL PARK

There isn't a team anywhere that hasn't played a game they've regretted. Joe Miller's famous line, "I shoulda stood in bed," says it all.

But four college baseball coaches in Massachusetts took that advice too seriously, and it cost them their jobs.

It all began when Framingham State coach Mark Driscoll and Salem State coach Bill MacLeod entered into a winner-take-all agreement for a May 4, 1980, doubleheader. The winner of the first game would also be declared the winner of the second. The coaches then reported the double win to the newspapers, complete with scores and game details.

Framingham's Driscoll said that he had made similar deals with the coaches of Fitchburg State and Boston State. He admitted that the second games of doubleheaders weren't played and that scores and statistics were falsified.

Why did he make the deals? The games were meaningless, according to Driscoll, since three of the four teams had losing records.

THE TIGERS' REVENGE

When Memphis State met Delta State (Miss.) on April 19, 1978, the Tigers had their hitting clothes on. The nation's ninth-ranked college baseball team at the time, Memphis State scored 11 runs in the first inning, piled up a 26–0 lead after four innings, and, all told, bombed four Delta State pitchers for 41 hits. When the dust cleared, the Tigers had won, 39–3.

The Delta State coach, Boo Ferris, a former major-leaguer, took the shellacking calmly. "I've been in baseball since 1942. I don't ever remember anyone scoring 39 runs. I guess it was their day."

What turned Memphis State on? Could have been the 19–5 loss they suffered at the hands of Delta State only two days earlier!

AN EYE ON THE BALL

Hitting a baseball may be the single most difficult skill in sports. It takes quick hands and sharp eyes. All of which makes Paul O'Dea's major league accomplishments that much more impressive.

O'Dea played 163 games for the 1944 and 1945 Cleveland Indians. He hit .318 and .235. Not bad for a player who had lost an eye in a freak spring training accident in 1940.

BEGINNER'S LUCK

Hoyt **Wilhelm** pitched for 21 years in the major **leagues. B**lessed with a rubber arm and a super **knuckleba**ll, Wilhelm stayed in the big time until **he was** 49 years old.

But Hoyt**, like** most pitchers, remembers his times **at bat,** too. When Wilhelm broke in with the **New York** Giants, he slugged a home run in his **first** at-bat. And in 21 years, he never hit **another** one!

STRIKE TWO—YERRR OUT!

"I always dreamed about my first major league at-bat," said Dorian (Doe) Boyland. "I thought I might hit a grand slam homer. I even realized that I might strike out. But this was too much."

Boyland's debut with the Pittsburgh Pirates on September 4, 1978, *was* too much. He watched himself strike out—from the Pittsburgh bench.

It happened against the New York Mets. Boyland was batting against right-handed reliever Skip Lockwood. The pitcher quickly got two strikes on the batter. Then Met manager Joe Torre went to the mound. He replaced Lockwood with the left-hander Kevin Kobel. Pirate manager Chuck Tanner responded by replacing Boyland with Rennie Stennett. Kobel got Stennett to strike out, but the strike-out was credited to Boyland.

"In all my dreams," said Boyland, "I never thought I'd strike out on two strikes—and be watching from the dugout."

BLOCK THAT KICK?

Fans of the Reno Silver Sox and the Visalia Oaks of the Class A California State League might have been confused in 1978. When they picked up their morning papers and checked the scores, they probably thought their teams had turned to football.

In the first game of a three-game series,

Reno came out on top, 24–12. But Visalia pulled even in the second game, 27–17, and won the third, 14–7.

SEEING DOUBLE

For Jack Kucek, May 26, 1978, was a night to remember. A pitcher for the Iowa Oaks of the American Association, he allowed no hits in chalking up a 6–1 win.

Why was the night especially memorable for Kucek? Well, no-hitters don't happen every day. Or do they? On the same night, while Kucek was spinning his classic for Iowa, Silvio Martinez of Springfield, another American Association team, was pitching a no-hitter against Omaha. If anything, Martinez was even more impressive than Kucek. He faced only 29 batters (two above the minimum) in a 4–0 victory.

For Martinez, that was just the start. Right after the game, he was called up to the major leagues by the St. Louis Cardinals. Four nights later, in his first big league start, he stopped the New York Mets on only *one hit*! He thus became only the second big-leaguer to throw a one-hitter in his first major league start.

THE THREE-BASE HOMER

A homer is a homer is a homer. Except when it's only a triple. That's what happened to Lou Gehrig back in 1931.

The New York Yankees' "iron man" was at

the plate. His teammate, Lyn Lary, was on second base.

Gehrig slammed the pitch over the fence. Lary rounded third, then headed for the dugout instead of home plate. "I thought the ball had been caught," he explained later.

Gehrig, running with his head down, scooted around the bases. When he hit the plate, the opponents howled. "Gehrig is out for passing a runner," they said. And the umpires—correctly—agreed. Gehrig was given credit for a triple instead of a homer.

Was it important? It sure was. When the season ended, Gehrig wound up with 46 home runs, the same as teammate Babe Ruth. Except for the base-running disaster, Gehrig would have won the league championship with 47 four-baggers.

But 1931 wasn't a total loss for Lou. He batted in 184 runs, the league's top total ever. And it's still the American League record.

JUST FOR THE RUN OF IT

In baseball, it doesn't matter whether you win by one run or ten runs. Just ask the 1960 New York Yankees.

When the American League champs met the NL-leading Pittsburgh Pirates in the play-offs, their bats were on fire. In seven games, the New Yorkers scored 55 runs, an average of just under eight per game. The Bucs, potent sluggers themselves, managed just 27 runs, a hair less than four per game.

No contest, right? Nope. The Pirates won the championship anyway. The Yanks managed to bunch their runs into games where the Pirates had trouble scoring. New York won game two 16–3, then game three 10–0, and game six 12–0. That accounted for 38 of the New York runs and only three of Pittsburgh's.

The Pirates made the most of their runs, winning game one 6–4, game four 3–2, game five 5–2, and the deciding seventh game 10–9. In the finale, Buc second baseman Bill Mazeroski stroked a solo homer in the bottom of the ninth to bring the championship flag to Pittsburgh.

HAVE BAT, WILL TRAVEL

You know what they say about hitters' parks? What about home field advantage? Baseball players get a homey feeling when they're playing in familiar surroundings.

But none of the above applies to the immortal Rogers Hornsby. No matter where this Hall-of-Famer played, he was at home. Check these numbers:

From 1915 to 1926, Hornsby starred for (and eventually managed) the St. Louis Cardinals, leading the National League (and of course the team) in hitting six times.

In 1927, Hornsby became a New York Giant. His .361 average was the team's best.

In 1928, it was on to the Boston Braves. Any problems? Not for Hornsby. His .387 average was the team's (and the league's) best.

In 1929, the Chicago Cubs made Hornsby

one of theirs. Rogers responded with a team-high .380 bat mark.

Hornsby played with four National League teams and led all four in hitting. No one else can make that claim.

WHO ELSE?

A few eyebrows were raised—but only for a moment—when major league baseball presented its 1981 Robert O. Fishel Award. The plaque is given annually to an off-the-field baseball person who performs outstanding work in public relations. It is named for Bob Fishel, longtime baseball PR man and, since 1974, public relations director for the American League.

And why were the eyebrows raised? The 1981 winner was none other than Robert O. Fishel himself.

TRIPPED UP

The Chicago White Sox had their fans buzzing with a special Prize Day promotion at the end of the 1981 season. The ball club was offering all sorts of goodies to the folks who showed up at Comiskey Park.

Top prize: a two-week, all-expenses-paid vacation trip to Puerto Rico. A dandy way to end the season? You bet. But it didn't turn out quite the way the Sox planned it.

The winner was Julio Nogueras, a great baseball fan who was visiting Chicago. From where? You guessed it, from Puerto Rico!

WHICH WAY DID HE GO?

The New York Yankees are often called the "Bronx Bombers." But "Bronx Bumblers" might have been more appropriate after their base-running performance at the Minneapolis Metrodome on May 29, 1982.

Yankee veterans Bobby Murcer and Graig Nettles opened the second inning with back-to-back singles. The next batter, shortstop Roy Smalley, ran the count to 3 and 2. On the next pitch, Murcer took off for third and Nettles for second. Smalley swung and missed for strike three. One out.

Twins catcher Sal Butera fired the ball

down to third baseman Gary Gaetti. Murcer wasn't close to third. So Gaetti began chasing him back toward second. Murcer returned to second safely, only to find Nettles already there.

According to baseball rules, the base belonged to Murcer. So Nettles did the only thing he could—he started back toward first. Bad move. Gaetti zipped the ball to first baseman Kent Hrbek who tagged Nettles out. Two outs.

Meanwhile, Murcer, figuring it would take a while to get Nettles, had set out for third again. Another unwise choice. Hrbek whipped the ball to pitcher Terry Felton, who by this time was covering third. Felton tagged Murcer to complete this odd triple play.

"I don't understand it," said Yankee third-base coach Joe Altobelli. "We start the runners to keep out of a double play and end up with a triple play!"

INCOME TAXIS

Some baseball players go through their entire career without ever setting a record. But Feigerito Corona set one before he ever stepped onto the diamond.

In 1978, Corona was signed to play for the Utica Blue Jays, a minor-league club run by the Toronto Blue Jays. That meant Feigerito had to make his way from his home in the Dominican Republic to Utica, in upstate New York. It wasn't easy.

When he arrived in New York City, Corona could not locate his luggage, which contained his visa. To make matters worse, Corona spoke no English. He finally located his bags, but then he could not find his wife.

Whom did he find? New York City cab driver Victor Gonzalez, who also had problems with English. But Gonzalez did help Feigerito find Mrs. Corona.

Then the Coronas and Gonzalez set out for Utica, 240 miles away. Gonzalez flipped on the meter in his taxi. By the time the trio arrived at the Utica ball park, the fare was up to $393, an all-time baseball record.

It wasn't easy to explain the problem to Blue Jay team officials. But they agreed to pay the fare. There's no word on whether they tipped the driver.

SPIKING A RUMOR

The Baseball Hall of Fame in Cooperstown, N.Y., is filled with lots of old baseball souvenirs. In one section, for instance, are the spiked shoes used by some of the greatest base-stealers ever. Maury Wills's shoes are there. So are Lou Brock's. And so are Richie Zisk's.

"Richie Zisk?" you say. "He's much closer to the tortoise than the hare. Why, he stole only six bases in his first 10 *seasons*!"

You're right, of course. So how come his shoes are there along with speed demons like Brock and Wills? It's simple. When Seattle's

Julio Cruz tied an American League record by stealing 32 bases without being caught, the Hall of Fame asked Cruz to send them the shoes he wore. Somehow, Cruz was wearing his teammate Zisk's shoes that night. That's why you'll find the plodding Zisk in the fast company of some of baseball's best base-thieves.

LUMBER PARTY

Richie Zisk's shoes aren't the only borrowed pieces of equipment in the Baseball Hall of Fame.

People who go to see the bat Mickey Mantle used to hit his 500th major league home run in 1967 won't see Mickey's bat at all. The lumber on display belongs to his teammate Joe Pepitone. Mickey had borrowed it just before striding to the plate.

SHORT AND SWEET

If you can only play one major league game, you might as well do what John Paciorek did.

Paciorek, the older brother of major-leaguer Tom Paciorek, was signed as a 17-year-old three-sport high school athlete by the Houston Colt 45s. (They've since become the Astros.)

After spending the 1963 season in the minors, Paciorek was called up by the big club to play in the last game of the year. What did he do? Not much: He came to the plate five times. He singled three times and walked twice. He scored four runs and batted in three more. Not bad, eh? But John Paciorek never played another major league game.

Returned to the minors for the 1964 season, he injured his back and had to have an operation. He never regained his earlier form. He played two more years for Houston farms and two for Indian farm clubs. He finally retired in 1968.

John had only one brief shining moment in the major league sun. But no one has ever made more of it!

WE INTERRUPT TODAY'S GAME . . .

How many ways can a baseball game be stopped? There's rain, of course. And fog. And even a power failure, like the one that interrupted the sixth game of the 1981 World Series for nine minutes.

But there are others, too. A Milwaukee Brewer-New York Yankee game at Yankee Stadium in 1980 was stopped for eight minutes because of a dust storm.

The last Washington Senators game in Washington (1971) had to be stopped several times because fans poured out onto the field. Most of them were diehard Senator fans who wanted a souvenir before their team became the Texas Rangers.

Then there was the first game ever by the

Toronto Blue Jays in Toronto (1977). This time the problem was snow. Thanks to the artificial turf, the game didn't have to be called off. But before it could start, snow machines had to remove the white stuff from the field. "It was embarrassing," remembers one fan. "It's the first American League game in Canada, and there are the White Sox (the visitors) playing touch football on the diamond while the snow is being removed."

But maybe the best cancellation of all belongs to the Pittsburgh Pirates. The field covering at Three Rivers Stadium is operated by a machine, not by a grounds crew. That day, the machine uncovering the field got stuck halfway. No one could budge it. And since you can't play baseball on top of a field covering, the game had to be called off.

FOUR HE'S A JOLLY GOOD FELLOW

Lots of baseball players are superstitious. And if all-time home-run king Hank Aaron is among them, chances are his lucky number is four.

Try these on "four" size: Hank's uniform number was 44.

In four of his big league seasons, he smacked exactly 44 home runs.

He broke Babe Ruth's all-time record by hitting his 715th big league homer in the fourth inning of the fourth game of the season in the fourth month (April).

And his victim on that glorious night: Los Angeles Dodger lefty Al Downing, who also wore uniform number 44.

CALLING (TO) COLLECT

The losingest baseball team ever? The 1962 New York Mets. The first-year team, managed by the lovable Casey Stengel, made up for lousy pitching with awful hitting and no fielding. No wonder Casey's first words to his new team were: "Can anybody here play this game?" The answer was a resounding "No!"

Still, in losing 120 games, the Mets had their moments. Despite losing streaks of 13 and 17, the Mets once erupted for a 19–1 victory over the Chicago Cubs at Wrigley Field.

Later that day, a fan called a newspaper in Connecticut. "How many runs did the Mets score?" asked the fan.

"Nineteen," he was told.

"Really," said the disbelieving fan. "Did they win?"

MAKING EVERYONE HEALTHY

Back in 1916, when the American League had only eight teams, six of them finished with at least .500 winning percentages. A seventh, the Washington Senators, just missed, finishing at .497.

How did seven teams do so well? They all

got healthy on number eight—the Philadel-phia Athletics. Owner-manager Connie Mack's A's were horrible. Pitcher Johnny Nabors won his first game, then lost his next 19. Other pitchers, like Tom Sheehan (1-16) and Jing Johnson (1-10), were just as unfortunate.

The A's gloves weren't much better. Third-sacker Charlie Peck weighed in with 42 errors. But he was a Golden Glover compared to shortstop Whitey Witt. Whitey booted 78 balls during the long season.

Put 'em all together and the spell D-I-S-A-S-T-E-R and a 36-117 season record.

ONE BRIEF SHINING MOMENT

Connie Mack's record may never be broken. Connie managed the Philadelphia Athletics from 1901 through 1950. Right, that's 50 sea-sons. Were the A's always good? They were not. In fact, they were often at the bottom of the American League standings.

So how did Connie hang on to his job? Sim-ple. He owned the ball club. The only man who could fire Connie was Connie.

At the other end of the tenure scale was Ed-die Stanky. A longtime, tough, major league infielder and later a reasonably successful manager, Stanky left the big league scene in 1968 and took over as coach at the University of South Alabama.

But he still had the big league bug. When the Texas Rangers invited him to run their club in 1977, he jumped at the chance—for a couple of days!

Eddie managed two games, won them both, and then quit. "I was lying in bed in my hotel," Eddie says, and I realized I didn't want to spend any more days on the road away from home."

THE UPSTARTS

No one believed the 1969 New York Mets. And with good reason. The Amazin' Mets were baseball's biggest laugh from their first day in 1962. When they finally climbed out of the National League basement in 1968, they moved all the way up to next to last (ninth place).

So their 1969 performance shocked the baseball world. The Metsies ran down all their competition in the newly formed National League East, then swept the Atlanta Braves in the first NL playoffs.

The American League champion Baltimore Orioles were expected to end the Mets' dreams in the World Series. And when Baltimore took game one, it seemed as though reality would return to baseball. But the Mets had some more miracles. They won the next four games and easily whipped the Maryland Birds.

When you're hot, you're hot, the Mets found out. Take back-up shortstop Al Weis. A seldom-used sub, Weis struggled through the '69 season, hitting only .215. But pressed into World Series service, Al became a madman at the plate. He swatted the ball at a .455 pace and became one of New York's many heroes.

But by the middle of the 1970 season, Weis had returned to his old ways. After playing in only 11 games, Weis was released in July.

SINGING OFF PITCH

When you talk about baseball "lumber companies," the 1930 Philadelphia Phillies are right up with the best. The Phils could hit with anyone, ringing up a .315 *team* batting average for the season. These days, a team is lucky to have one or two .300 hitters.

So how did the Phils make out? They finished last. Trouble was, their pitchers couldn't get anyone out. Philly hurlers were touched up for a season 6.71 earned run average, about double what a team needs to win a championship.

IT MAY STILL BE ROLLING

The two greatest sluggers of all time, Hank Aaron and Babe Ruth, smacked 1,469 homers between them. Most were of the classic variety, long and high, shots that awed their fans.

Neither ever hit a homer like George Cutshaw did for the 1913 Brooklyn Dodgers. Fact is, no other player ever did.

In the bottom of the eleventh, he stroked a Phillie pitch down the right-field line. As the ball sailed toward the wall in right, Cutshaw rounded first and headed for second. The Philadelphia right-fielder chased the ball to the fence and waited for the rebound. He knew he'd have to make a good throw to get Cutshaw at second.

But there was no rebound. The fates were smiling on the Dodgers and Cutshaw that day. Instead of hitting the wall and bouncing back, the ball kept climbing the wall. Up, up it went, until it cleared the top of the fence and fell into the street behind Ebbets Field. And, under 1913 rules, any ball that cleared the fence in fair territory, no matter how it got over, was a home run.

George Cutshaw had hit the only ground ball homer in baseball history.

THE BOSTON MIRACLE

Every few years, baseball seems to come up with a miracle team. There were the Miracle Giants of 1951, the Miracle Mets of 1969, and lots of others.

But perhaps the biggest miracle ever was turned in by the 1914 Boston Braves.

In mid-July the Bostonians were limping along in last place, 11½ games behind the league-leading Giants.

That's when the miracle began. The Braves reeled off 59 wins in their last 75 games to pass their seven National League rivals and take the pennant.

They'd meet their match in the World

Series, cautioned the experts. The Philadelphia A's would be too much.

Wrong again! The miracle kept right on working. Philadelphia's Eddie Collins, a .344 hitter, batted .214 for the Series. Rube Oldring, a .277 hitter, batted .067. And Braves catcher Hank Gowdy went on a rampage and hit .545. The Miracle Bostonians swept the powerful A's in four straight, 7–1, 1–0, 5–4, and 3–1.

TWO FOR ONE

When the Boston Red Sox invaded New York's Yankee Stadium on September 28, 1951, the home team stood only one win from clinching a tie for its third consecutive American League title.

In such an important contest, the New Yorkers went with their best pitcher, right-handed Allie Reynolds, who had pitched a no-hit, no-run game early in the season.

Reynolds was never better, mowing down the Sox inning after inning. As he strode to the mound to begin the ninth, he stood only three outs away from becoming the first American League pitcher to twirl two no-hitters in one season.

The crowd of 40,000-plus moved closer to the edges of their seats. Quickly, Reynolds retired the first two Sox batters. Now only one man stood between Reynolds and his no-hitter.

But the one man was Ted Williams, one of baseball's all-time great hitters.

Reynolds bent in for the sign from his catcher, Yogi Berra. Then he delivered a quick strike past the Boston slugger. He pitched again. This time Williams swung, lofting a high pop foul to the right of home plate. As the fans held their breath, Berra camped under the ball and tossed his mask away. Then at the last instant the ball blew away from him. He lunged for it, but it skipped off his glove. Yogi sprawled in the dirt. Williams was still alive.

Reynolds raced over to his fallen teammate. "Don't worry, Yog! We'll get him on the next pitch," he said.

How right he was! On the next delivery, Williams again lofted a pop foul near the plate. Berra camped under this one as the fans stood. This time the ball plopped right down into Yogi's glove. He squeezed it tight and the game was over. Reynolds had his no-hitter.

The Yanks went on to take the pennant and their third straight World Series.

LINGERING INJURY

There was some concern around Fenway Park when former Red Sox pitching star Smokey Joe Wood (34-5 in 1912) was asked to throw out the first ball of the 1982 season.

Some fans were worried about Wood's age. At the time, he was 92.

That didn't bother Wood, though. He was more concerned about his throwing arm. "It locks on me from time to time," said the aging star, "ever since I hurt it."

And when was that, Joe?

"If I remember correctly," he responded, "it was sometime during the 1913 season."

UP, UP, AND AWAY

Every baseball player dreams of wearing the hero's crown at the World Series. For Pittsburgh's John Miljus, the fourth game of the 1927 Series nearly gave him that opportunity.

With the score tied at 3–3 in the ninth inning, the rival Yankees loaded the bases, with no outs. The next three Yankee hitters? Lou Gehrig, Bob Muesel, and Tony Lazzeri—that's all!

Miljus took a deep breath and struck out Gehrig. One out. Then he whiffed Meusel. Two out. The crowd roared.

Lazzeri came to the plate. Miljus threw the first pitch for a strike. Again he delivered. The ball went up, up—and over the catcher's head. The runner on third raced across the plate and the Series was over.

Miljus, almost the hero, slowly walked off as the goat.

I'LL HUFF AND I'll PUFF . . .

What do Bert Haas and Len Randle have in common? To start with, they both have a powerful set of lungs.

Bert displayed his baseball wisdom first. In a 1940 game against the Jersey City Giants (International League), Montreal third base-man Haas was playing at normal depth with Giant runners on first and second.

When the Giant batter bunted beautifully down the third-base line, Haas knew he had to do something. The Giant runner on second had already turned third and was headed for the plate as the ball continued to roll down the line.

Springing into action, Haas raced to the ball, got down on all fours, and, blowing with all his might, steered the ball into foul territory. As soon as he touched the ball, the umpire ruled it a foul, thus canceling the run which had already scored.

Randle is obviously a student of history. Playing for the Seattle Mariners 40 years later, Randle was confronted with a similar situation. His reaction was identical to Haas's. And so were Lenny's results. Just one more wind-blown foul bunt.

ALL THROUGH THE NIGHT

When the Pawtucket pitcher arrived home at 2 A.M., his wife was waiting for him.

"Where have you been?" she asked angrily.

"At the ball park," he answered.

"Aw, c'mon," she said. "The game started at 8 o'clock."

"It's true," he responded. "As a matter of fact, they're still playing."

Fortunately, the pitcher's wife waited until the morning to do her husband any bodily harm. By then she'd read the morning paper and found her husband's "tale" was right on the money.

The Pawtucket Red Sox and the Rochester Red Wings of the International League had gone to work at 8 P.M. on April 18, 1981. By the time they knocked off for the evening, it was 4:07 A.M. on Easter Sunday morning, April 19. In the eight hours plus, the teams had played 32 innings to a 2–2 tie.

It started innocently enough. The teams played six scoreless innings before Rochester pushed over a run. They held the 1–0 lead into the bottom of the ninth when Pawtucket knotted the score.

Inning after inning, the clubs hung zero after zero on the scoreboard. Rochester finally put together a "rally" in the 21st and scored one run. Perhaps the already long night would come to an end. But Pawtucket thought otherwise. They matched the run in the bottom of the 21st. With the score tied at 2–2, the zeroes continued.

By 4 A.M. only 47 of the original 1,740 fans were still in the stands. Pawtucket management was dispensing free coffee to everyone and presented each of the hardy souls a free season ticket.

At 4:07, after 32 innings, the umpires called a halt to the proceedings. Apparently, the game had gone three hours beyond the legal "closing time." When Pawtucket officials got in touch with the league president, they were informed that the game was covered by a league curfew rule. "When the next inning ends," ordered the president, "suspend the game."

The finish was postponed until the next time Rochester visited Pawtucket, on June 23. This time, 6,000 curious fans were on hand. Rochester was retired quickly. Then, in the bottom of the 33rd, Pawtucket second base-- man Marty Barrett was hit by a pitch. Left- fielder Chico Walker lined a single to the cen- ter, sending Barrett to third. Designated hitter Russ Laribee was intentionally walked, filling the bases. That brought up Dave Koza, who banged out his fifth hit of the interrupted game to score Barrett with the winning run.

It took only 18 minutes for Koza to knock in the game-winner. And the losing pitcher? He was Rochester's Steve Grilli. His memory of the eight-hour game was just a little fuzzy. When it started back in April, he was pitching for Syracuse!

LOW CALORIE GAME

Baseball games have been called off for a large variety of reasons—everything from rain and snow to power failures.

But when the college game between Pem- broke State and North Carolina-Charlotte ended in an 8–8 tie during March 1982, a new excuse had been created. The game was called because of hunger.

"It was 6:25," said Pembroke coach Harold Ellen. "Our cafeteria closes at 6:30. And I couldn't afford to have our players eat in a restaurant. So that was it. Besides, after you've played nine innings in three and a half hours, that's really enough baseball."

NO HITS, NO WIN

It was just one of those days for Chicago
Cub pitcher Hippo Vaughn. The Cubs' star
left-hander was throwing nothing but aspirin
tablets at the Cincinnati Reds. As the innings
flew by, not one Red batter had managed a hit
in the 1917 game.

Unfortunately, his teammates couldn't
manage a hit, either. Cincy's Fred Toney was
just as effective.

Through nine innings, both pitchers were
near-perfect. Vaughn was overpowering,
striking out 10 Reds and not allowing a runner farther than first. Toney had allowed only
one Cubbie as far as second base. They had
combined for the only double no-hitter in
baseball history.

In overtime, however, Toney was stronger.
Vaughn gave up a single to Cincy shortstop
Larry Kopf. A dropped fly ball allowed Kopf
to move to third. He scored on an infield single by Jim Thorpe.

Toney then retired the Cubs in the bottom
of the tenth to sew up his end of the no-hitter
with a 1–0 win.

PLAY IT AGAIN,
DIFFERENTLY

The most talked-about sporting event in
Chicago in 1979? No doubt about it. It was the

Phillies' rip-roaring 23–22 victory over the Cubs. (Yes, they were playing baseball.)

The crowd at Wrigley Field loved everything except the final score. And the game really tickled the fancy of Chicagoland TV watchers. As they came home from work, they were amazed to find the game still going on. And they stayed glued to their sets until the final Cub out was recorded.

The Cubs' TV station, WGN-TV, didn't forget. When snow and ice covered Chicago's windy streets in January 1980, the station decided to provide a touch of springtime.

With much fanfare, WGN replayed the entire telecast. The fans, well aware of the result, still tuned in—just to remember. But the station had a surprise for them.

Right after Phillie Mike Schmidt's game-winning homer gave Philadelphia its 23–22 margin, announcer Jack Brickhouse broke in and said, "Yes, that was the way it happened. But wouldn't it have been nice if . . ."

Suddenly, the legendary Ernie Banks, known as "Mr. Cub," appeared on the screen in a film of an earlier game. Thanks to the magic of television, Banks smashed a two-run homer and Chicago "won" the replay, 24–23!

FOOT-IN-MOUTH DISEASE

Did you ever say anything you wish you could take back? Of course. But no one ever regretted it like Bill Terry, manager of the then New York Giants.

Midway through the 1934 season, reporters asked Terry for his opinion of his team's arch-rivals, the Brooklyn Dodgers, managed by Casey Stengel.

"The Dodgers?" scoffed Terry. "Is Brooklyn still in the league?"

Terry got his answer during the final series of the season. With the Giants poised to win the National League pennant, Brooklyn upset New York over the last weekend of the season and gave the flag to the St. Louis Cardinals.

Brooklyn then stayed in the league, much to Bill Terry's regret, until they moved to Los Angeles in 1958.

FOOTBALL
FUMBLES

GET 'EM, GIRLS

"Betty takes the snap, fakes to Mona, gives to Joyce. There's a big hole. First down."

An all-girl football team? Hardly. Just a routine running play for the University of Maryland's 1959 grid squad. Quarterback Dale Betty and running backs Joe Mona and Jim Joyce helped lead the Terps to a 5–5 season (after three straight losing campaigns).

And they got plenty of respect, too. Joyce was the Atlantic Coast Conference's leading rusher.

ALL IN A DAY'S WORK

Two-a-day workouts are routine preseason fare for pro football players. But when the two workouts are held 3,700 miles apart, you've got something special.

The San Diego Chargers pulled off the long-distance feat on a Thursday back in 1976. San Diego was in the midst of a two-game preseason road trip, with games scheduled in Tokyo,

Japan, and Honolulu, Hawaii.

Before departing from Japan, the Chargers held a workout on Thursday afternoon. Then they boarded a Thursday night flight, which crossed the International Date Line and got them to Hawaii on Thursday *morning*. After a couple of hours of sleep, the Chargers were back on the field for their second Thursday afternoon practice.

DON'T CALL US . . .

After 60 minutes, the Dallas Texans and Houston Oilers were tied. At stake: the 1962 American Football League championship.

As the officials got set to toss the coin to start the overtime period, Texan coach Hank Stram called his captain, Abner Haynes, to his side.

"There's a powerful wind," said the coach. "If we win the toss, we want the wind. That means we'll kick off toward the scoreboard clock."

"Got it, coach," said Haynes as he raced toward midfield.

The Texans won the toss. "Your choice, captain," said the referee to Haynes.

"We'll kick to the clock," said Haynes.

"Are you sure that's what you want to do?" said the official.

"Yup," said Haynes again, "we'll kick to the clock."

"Your first choice is the one," said the ref. "Dallas will kick. Houston has the choice of direction."

Naturally, the Oilers took the wind at their back. Haynes had goofed. Dallas had neither the ball nor the wind.

Stram was furious. But he couldn't do a thing about it. Fortunately, his players could. They held Houston for 15 minutes; then, three minutes into the second overtime period, with the wind at their back, the Texans kicked the winning field goal.

HOMER RUN

Homer Hazel was a one-man wrecking crew for Rutgers U. in 1923. Homer, blessed with sprinter speed, was also the Rutgers kicker. He put the two skills together to rack up one of the quickest touchdowns ever.

Playing against Villanova, Homer kicked off to start the game. The Wildcats bobbled the ball in the end zone. Hazel came streaking down the field and recovered the loose ball for a Rutgers touchdown.

Time elapsed: only eight seconds between Hazel's kick and Hazel's TD.

SAFETY LAST

Though the coaches would disagree, football isn't usually called "the thinking man's game." But the lack of thought can sometimes prove costly.

Witness the case of Rick Gervais, a kick returner for Stanford U. during the 1979 season.

Oregon State had just tied the Cardinals at 31–31. The Beavers' kickoff came tumbling down to Gervais at the Stanford one-yard line.

Without thinking, Gervais caught the ball, took one step back into the end zone, and kneeled. He thought the officials would rule a touchback, which would give Stanford the ball on its 20.

However, the referee correctly ruled that Gervais had brought the ball into the end zone (it hadn't been kicked that far), and Oregon State was awarded a safety—and two points.

The Beavers held on to win, 33–31.

DENNY, GO HOME

Stanford's Rick Gervais isn't the only player to cost his team through faulty kick-running.

In a 1905 game against the U. of Chicago, Michigan's Denny Clark was tackled in his end zone trying to return a punt. The safety gave the Chicago team two points, all they needed to win the game, 2–0.

The press and Clark's schoolmates showed no mercy. One newspaper headline read: "Clark 2, Michigan 0." His fellow students refused to speak to him.

Within one week, Clark had quit school.

GRIN AND BEAR IT

Bear Bryant's teams usually leave nothing to doubt. But when the Bear was coaching at Kentucky, there was a moment or two . . .

Bear's Wildcats were playing against Tennessee, their arch-rivals. There was a fumble in front of the Kentucky bench. Suddenly there were footballs all over the field.

"The players were scrambling for the loose ball," remembers the Bear. "Somehow they knocked over a box with eight more balls in it. No one could tell which one was the game

39

ball. There were players on top of each of the nine balls."

How did the officials sort out the damage?

"They counted up," says Bryant. "Tennessee had five balls and we had only four. The refs gave the ball to Tennessee."

HAIL TO THE REDSKINS

Do Washington Redskins fans take their football seriously? You know it. Despite the team's so-so performances over the last 30 years, a 'Skins ticket is still the hottest item in town.

Need more proof? Check this story. When an unnamed Redskin fan died suddenly during the midst of the 1979 season, his wife began to make funeral arrangements. Scheduling dictated that the services be held on Sunday, November 11. But that was the day of the Washington Redskins-St. Louis Cardinals game. In order not to inconvenience the football fans, the widow postponed the funeral to Monday, November 12. The widow's patience was rewarded. Washington won, 30–28. And the next day, more than 500 friends showed up at the funeral.

IN A HURRY

Yogi Berra said it: "The game ain't over till it's over." He was almost right.

In the very first Rose Bowl game (1902), Stanford was having a bad time of it. Facing Michigan's undefeated (10-0), untied, and unscored upon (501-0) Wolverines, the Stanford team trailed 49–0 at the end of the third quarter.

With 15 minutes still to play, things didn't look too bright for the Indians. So as they approached the line of scrimmage to begin the fourth period, they shouted across to Michigan: "We're ready to quit, if you're willing." The Wolverines were happy to.

So if you think that football is a 60-minute game, remember the 1902 Rose Bowl, the first and only 45-minute contest in the Bowl's history.

THE STRANGE GREY CUP

Canada's version of the Super Bowl is called The Grey Cup. It's supposed to match the two best teams in Canadian professional football, and it usually does.

But that doesn't mean that the game doesn't sometimes take strange twists and turns.

They called the 1950 Grey Cup The Mud Bowl. The game was played in Toronto. A blanket of eight inches of snow had turned the field into a giant sea of mud. It was no joke. During the game, the Winnipeg Blue Bombers' giant 268-pound tackle Bud Tinsley was knocked unconscious. He fell facedown in a mud puddle. It took quick work to prevent him from drowning.

The Blue Bombers were involved in another weirdo in 1962. Fog had rolled in off Lake Ontario. Visibility was near zero. When the Winnipeg quarterback dropped back and fired a perfect strike—right to one of the officials—they decided to postpone the rest of the game to another day.

The 1977 Grey Cup was played in Montreal. A sheet of ice had covered the field. (Montreal officials flood the field after every football season anyway, and it's used as one of Canada's biggest outdoor skating rinks.) Traction was impossible. Players were sliding all over the field. Finally, one of the Montreal Alouettes' players had an idea. He drove staples into the bottoms of his shoes. He did the same for his teammates. It must have been a great idea. Montreal defeated the Edmonton Eskimos 41–6.

THE WORM TURNED

Talk about weird postgame shows. California State (Sacramento) linebacker Dave Mondragon had the weirdest ever. After every Cal State win, Dave swallowed a live fishing worm for every point his team scored. Bad enough, right? But even Dave had a severe problem when the Hornets blew out the U. of San Francisco. The score: 47–0.

Pass the salt and pepper, please.

CHANGE OF DIRECTION

Craig Ward would just as soon forget the night of September 19, 1980. The punter for Cortez (Colo.) High School, Craig had his first kick blocked. So as he lined up for his second punt, he concentrated extra hard.

He took the snap, moved forward, dropped the ball, and booted it. His form was beautiful. "I thought it was the world's best punt," he said later. "But I didn't know where it went after I kicked it."

That's not surprising. Craig's punt traveled 38 yards—the wrong way! In all, Craig punted

43

four times in the game, for an average of only two and a half yards. Cortez must have been pretty tough, however. They still managed to tie Aztec (N.M.) High School 6–6.

INSTANT REPLAY

Has television taken over sports? That's what some writers and fans say. If they need proof, they point to the 1980 football meeting between Penn State and Texas A&M at College Station, Tex.

Penn State won the toss and elected to receive the opening kickoff. The A&M kicker moved into the ball and booted a long, twisting kick that sailed over the end line. Touchback. Penn State ball at the 20.

Then the referee blew his whistle and called both teams together. The Penn State TV network was showing a commercial and missed the kickoff. "We'll have to do it again," said the referee.

And so they did. Fortunately for A&M, the kicker booted the ball out of the end zone again!

I DON'T WANT IT, EITHER

The pros of the National Football League are the greatest players in the world. But you'd have a tough time convincing the Green

Bay fans who sat in on the 1979 game between the Packers and the Oakland Raiders.

Four minutes into the second quarter, Oakland quarterback Ken Stabler dropped back and passed—right to Packer cornerback Willie Buchanon. Green Bay ball. But not for long.

On the Packs' first play, quarterback David Whitehurst set up and passed—right to Oakland linebacker Phil Villapiano. It was Whitehurst's first interception in three games that season.

So Oakland got the ball back, just in time for Stabler to pass to Green Bay linebacker Mike Hunt.

This time, the Packers kept the ball for *two* plays. Whitehurst rolled to his right and lateraled the ball. But the Green Bay runner wasn't there. Mr. Villapiano was there again and he picked the ball up on the Oakland 49.

This time Oakland settled down, and four plays later Stabler hit Dave Casper for a touchdown. The Raiders went on to win 28–3. But the four turnovers in just over one minute left everyone wondering who these two "high school" teams really were.

ONE FOR THE BOOKS

The 1935 Notre Dame-Northwestern football game matched two of the "stars" of literature. Notre Dame featured a running back named William Shakespeare. Northwestern used an end named Henry Wadsworth Longfellow.

The two "poets" didn't fare badly. Shakespeare was a key in Notre Dame's success early in the game. The Irish led 7–0 as the fourth quarter began.

But Longfellow was not to be outdone. He grabbed a touchdown pass early in the final period to tie the game. His Wildcats then went on to win 14–7.

HISTORY REPEATS

The Miami Dolphins played their first ever regular-season pro contest on September 2, 1966. Their AFL opponents: the Oakland Raiders.

Oakland kicked off to start the game. Miami's Joe Auer grabbed the ball at his own five-yard line and carried it all the way—95 yards for a Dolphin touchdown. Not a bad way to start a franchise. But the play apparently woke up the Raiders. They went on to win 23–14.

One year later, the New Orleans Saints opened up their doors for the first time. Their opponents: the Los Angeles Rams. L.A. kicked off to start the game. New Orleans' John Gilliam grabbed the ball at his own six-yard line and carried it all the way—94 yards for a Saint touchdown. Not a bad way to start a franchise. But history does teach us a few lessons. The Rams were also awakened by the play. They went on to win 27–13.

ALL THAT FOR TWO POINTS

Everett Newcomb, a junior high school football coach in Bernardsville, N.J., was thrilled when his team moved 60 yards in seven plays for its first touchdown of the 1977 season.

Newcomb decided to go for a two-point conversion and called a power sweep to the right. The halfback swept across the goal line, but the team was called for holding. The officials moved the ball back to the 18-yard line. This time Newcomb called a power sweep to the left. His team scored again, but this time they were called for clipping. The ball went back to the 33-yard line.

"Let's try a long pass to our wide receiver," said Newcomb to his quarterback. And it worked like a charm. His team scored again. Uh-oh. Another flag. The penalty was for holding—again. The ball went back to the 48-yard line.

"The boys were becoming confused," remembers Newcomb. "I thought we'd better do something simple. I wanted to get it over with. I called a fullback dive, a play designed to gain three or four yards."

What happened? You guessed it. The fullback went all the way, and this time there were no penalties.

The 48-yard extra point may have been the longest ever.

DESIGNATED COACH

It was the worst of times for Susquehanna University and its football team. The squad was awful—and getting worse. The president of the university, Gustave Weber, decided that something had to be done.

His second move was a little more suprising. He decided to lead by example. He appointed *himself* as head football coach.

His first move was not unexpected. He asked the coaching staff to resign. They did.

The results? Coach Weber lost his first two games, fired himself, and went back to running the university.

HEADS I WIN ...

San Diego University usually has an out-standing football team. But no matter how hot the Aztecs get, they'll be hard pressed to match their record for winning the toss of the coin. San Diego won the toss 15 straight times. How difficult is that? According to oddsmakers, the chances of that happening are about 33,000-to-1.

DOUBLE ERROR

What's the worst thing a football player can do? Run the ball the wrong way—toward his own goal line. But what act is even worse? Tackling the wrong-way runner.

The most famous wrong-way runner ever was Roy Riegels. His goof cost his California team a safety and gave Georgia Tech an 8–7 win in the 1929 Rose Bowl.

The same thing happened to a halfback named Dickinson who played for Rutgers in 1922. But he was saved from Riegels's fate— by his opponents.

In a game at Morgantown, W. Va., Dickinson corralled a West Virginia fumble and took off—for his own goal line. He'd gone about 20 yards in the wrong direction when he was smeared by two West Virginians, Charlie Howard and All-American Joe Setron.

HAVEN HELP US

Old-time Georgia Tech fans get a little chuckle when they recall the Engineers' 220–0 victory over tiny Cumberland College in 1916. It was the worst mismatch in college football history.

But the 1928 Sylvia (Kan.) High School team could symphathize with Cumberland. On a bright autumn afternoon, they were "murdered" in broad daylight by a team from

Haven High, 256–0. All but one of the 30 players on the Haven squad scored at least one touchdown.

But Sylvia had lots of company. Haven defeated all nine opponents, outscoring its rivals 578–0.

OFFICIAL SCORER

Houston (Tex.) Central High and Yates High were all locked up, 13–13, as time began to run out. Yates had the ball on its own 13-yard line and, as they put the ball into play, the referee dropped his flag.

When the whistle blew, the ref marched over to the ball, signaled a 15-yard penalty against Yates, and marked off the yardage—two yards into the Yates end zone. He placed the ball down and raised his arms, signaling a safety. The two points gave Central an unbelievable 15–13 win.

BEARS' COMPUTER

The 1940 National Football League championship game shaped up as a classic. It matched pro football's two best teams, the Washington Redskins and the Chicago Bears. Each team had a super quarterback—Sammy Baugh of Washington and Sid Luckman of Chicago. When the two clubs played three weeks earlier, Washington took a hard-fought 7–3 victory.

But the best-laid plans of mice, men, and football teams often go astray. The Bears made up for their earlier defeat. Oh, how they made up for it! Final score: Bears 73, 'Skins 0.

The first play from scrimmage gave promise of things to come. Luckman handed to Bill Osmanski, who swept around end and raced 63 yards to score. Only 55 seconds had been played.

The Redskins came right back and threatened to score. Unfortunately, a perfect pass by Baugh was dropped into the end zone.

The rest of the game was all Chicago. Luckman scored on a sneak and Joe Maniaci tallied on another long TD sprint. The Bears led 21–0 after the first quarter.

The 'Skins were so far behind in the second half that they were forced to throw on nearly every down. Chicago returned three third-quarter interceptions for touchdowns.

The Bears kicked so many extra points that the 'Skins began to run out of footballs. Chicago owner-coach George Halas did what he could. He had his team run for the extra points.

When the game ended, reporters gathered around Sammy Baugh's locker. "What would have happened," they asked, "if your first-quarter pass had been caught?"

The Washington star never hesitated. "We'd have lost 73–7!"

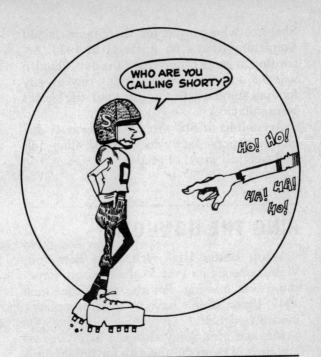

OR WAS HE A TALL MIDGET?

When 5-4, 168-pound Reggie Smith started carrying back kicks for the Atlanta Falcons, pro football historians started searching for other tiny pros. And they found a few.

One-time Kansas City kick-returner Nolan Smith was only 5-6. Mack Herron and Howard Stevens were part of a small group at 5-5. And all-timer Buddy Young, now an NFL executive, was only 5-4½.

But the smallest ever may have been Jack

Shapiro, who played for the Staten Island Stapletons (that's no mistake) in 1929. According to game programs of the day, Shapiro was 5-5 and 130 pounds. That's tiny by any football standard. But, it turns out, the figures were inflated.

According to Shapiro's World War II discharge papers, Jack was no more than 5-0½ and weighed just 119 pounds.

RING THE GONGOLA

When Union High School in Benwood, W. Va., opened its 1966 football season, something was missing. For the first time since 1941, Union didn't have at least one player named Gongola.

Mr. and Mrs. Andy Gongola had 12 sons, and each of them did their bit for Union. First came Emil, then Joe, then Anthony, Vic, John, Pete, Tom, Ed, Fred, Stanley, Frank, and finally Herman.

When Herman, a 240-pound fullback, played his last game, Union's athletic department decided to honor the entire family. The parents were given a color television set in gratitude for their contribution.

Then the game began, and the Gongolas sat back to watch. That was a great thrill for Mrs. Gongola. Although her sons had played in every Union game for 24 seasons—more than 200 games—it was the first one she'd ever attended.

(K)NEEDLESS WASTE

His players may get uptight. But a high school football coach is supposed to stay loose.

Things don't always work out that way. Coach Lou Goldstein's Carter Riverside (Fort Worth, Tex.) team was all keyed up to play Texarkana High. So was Goldstein.

Just prior to kickoff, Goldstein gathered his squad around him and asked if there were any questions. One player, suffering from a knee injury, piped up: "Yes, coach. Why did you tape the wrong knee?"

BASKETBALL
BLOOPERS

UNREWARDING VICTORY

Although Davidson College (Davidson, N.C.) has a rich basketball tradition, the Wildcats suffered through a terrible 1980 season. They finished last in the Southern Conference.

But 1981 was different. Coach Eddie Biedenbach led his team all the way back. The 'Cats 11-5 record got them a tie for first in the league.

What was Biedenbach's reward? He was fired.

JOINT PROBLEM

After coaching 823 college games, Rockford (Ill.) College coach Chuck DeWild thought he had seen everything. Then came game number 824, against Northeastern Illinois, and DeWild found out that you're never too old to learn.

Just before game time, DeWild learned that his top reserve, Brian Andrews, had the flu. Not to worry. The starters were okay. And the teams played the first half just about even.

The second half was another story. Guard Ted Fritz sprained his ankle. Then center Don Bentz had to leave with a back injury. By the midpoint of the half, two other starters had sprained their ankles and were done.

By the end of the game, coach DeWild was down to his subs' subs. Going down the stretch, his players tried hard but could only hit on four of their last 19 shots. Northeastern Illinois's 77–67 victory came as no surprise.

SELECT CIRCLE

Every sport has its special numbers: a .300 batting average in baseball, a four-minute mile in track, 50 goals in ice hockey.

In pro basketball, 500 wins for a coach is a magic number. That's why the night of November 20, 1979, stands as a big one in the National Basketball Association.

First, in New York's Madison Square Garden, the Knicks beat the Houston Rockets, 130–125 in overtime. The special event: Coach Red Holzman's 500th win as Knick coach.

A couple of hours later, in Portland, the Trail Blazers downed the Los Angeles Lakers, 114–99. The special event: Coach Jack Ramsay's 500th victory as an NBA coach.

A half-hour later the results were in from San Diego. The Clippers had beaten the Phoenix Suns, 117–110. A big deal? You bet. It was the 500th NBA coaching victory for Clipper bench boss Gene Shue.

POINTS OF ORDER

Basketball has its share of three-point plays with occasional four-point plays. But an 11-point play? It happened a couple of seasons back in Saddleback, Cal.

Saddleback College was leading San Diego City College 79–69 with 11:30 to go. It started innocently enough. As Saddleback's Artie Green sank a lay-up, referee Al Hackney called a foul on San Diego's Al Brown. Brown went crazy and began arguing long and loud with the ref. Hackney called three technical fouls on Brown before tossing him out of the game.

This didn't sit too well with San Diego coach Caldwell Black. When he chimed in on the discussion, Hackney hit him with a technical as well. Finally, Artie Green went to the line and missed his shot (on Brown's original foul). But his teammate, Tim Shaw, sank seven in a row on the technical fouls.

Then Saddleback got the ball out of bounds and converted a field goal. The two baskets and seven foul shots added up to 11 points. In a matter of seconds, Saddleback's lead had gone from 79–69 to 90–69. That was all she wrote for San Diego. Saddleback went on to win 140–102.

What about the Saddleback coach, Bill Mulligan? He sat on the sidelines, taking in the whole scene. "I've been coaching 20 years," he said, "and I've never seen anything like it." Neither had anyone else.

ONE FOR ALL

The outlook was kind of gloomy for University Lake H.S. (Hartland, Wis.) one winter day in 1978. The school's girls' basketball team was slated to play Shoreland Lutheran H.S. in Kenosha, Wis. And four of the nine University Lake players were out with the flu. That left just five girls to play the entire game.

The quintet played a near-perfect first half. Despite their limited numbers, they led 22–11 at the break. Then things got worse.

First, University Lake's Mary Allen fouled out. The team was down to four players. Still, by the end of the third quarter they were still on top, 25–16.

Then Rita Landis sprained her ankle early in the fourth quarter. University Lake was down to three players. When Sandy Saeger fouled out with just under three minutes left and Ann Yeomans fouled out with a minute to go, University Lake was down to only one player. Still, they led 33–25.

So now it was Laura Merisalo against Shoreland Lutheran. It wasn't easy. It was hard enough for her to play defense against five opponents. It was even harder for her to throw the ball in from out of bounds. (She had to toss the ball to an opponent and hope to steal it back.)

How did Laura do? Just fine, thank you. Though she gave up four points in the final minute, University Lake hung on to win 33–29.

WARPED SENSE OF HOMER

When is a home court advantage not a home court advantage? When you're playing at home but not on your home court.

Sound strange? Here are the details. The Philadelphia 76ers returned from an eight-game road trip, all set to play the Boston Celtics. The date: March 7, 1979. While the Sixers were away, the Ice Capades had been using their arena, the Spectrum. Meanwhile, the team's basketball court had been stored away—but not well. When the arena crew tried to set it up, they found that rain and snow had seeped into the storage room and warped the court.

The Sixers knew what to do. They put in an emergency call to the Philadelphia Civic Center, whose court had been tucked away neatly since the team last used it—11 years earlier. Must have been some magic left, because the Sixers downed the Celtics, 114–107.

So why wasn't this a home court advantage for Philadelphia? Because most of the players were still in junior high school the last time it had been used!

ALL DRESSED UP, NO PLACE TO PLAY

When the Colonel White H.S. team of Dayton, O., boarded the bus, they felt great.

White was 2-0 and they figured they'd have an easy time against Spencer-Sharples H.S. in Toledo.

The bus trip covered 150 miles and took three hours. And when the White team arrived, they went into shock. Little did they know that Spencer-Sharples H.S. was among 11 schools in Toledo that had been closed. A $4.3 million cut in the school budget had forced the closings.

"I was in shock," remembers White coach Neal Huysman. "We pulled up to the school— and no one was there. The school was all boarded up. It looked like a prison."

ACTUALLY, HE WAS UNDEFEATED

Can you believe a Coach of the Year who'd never won a game? That was the story in the Eastern Eight Basketball Conference in 1981.

Here's what happened: After leading Rhode Island to an opening game win, head coach Jack Kraft suffered a mild heart attack. His doctors told him he was through for the year.

But the Rams needed a coach. So they told associate coach Claude English to fill in for Kraft. Kraft, however, retained the title of head coach.

English enjoyed a dynamite season. By year's end, the Rams had a sparkling 20-6 record. But the wins and losses all went on Kraft's record. English, who later became the head coach, was still 0-0. That didn't stop his colleagues in the league from naming him Coach of the Year (along with Duquesne's Mike Rice).

DON'T CALL US . . .

Kevin Stacom, a veteran of the pro basketball wars, learned a valuable lesson on November 20, 1981. If you open your mouth, you might have to pay the price.

Stacom, retired from the NBA and part-owner of a Providence (R.I.) tavern, was having lunch in Boston with his old buddy and teammate, Don Nelson. Nelson, the coach of the Milwaukee Bucks, was crying the blues. "Injuries have ruined our backcourt," he said, between bites.

"What are you worried about?" kidded Stacom. "I can help out. I've been working out with my former teammates."

But it was no joking matter with Nelson. When he got back to his team's hotel, Nelson talked to his assistants, then called Stacom and told him to come to Boston Garden that night—ready to play!

And he did. In fact, the 30-year-old Stacom turned in 20 excellent minutes, hitting five of eight field goal tries.

ON THE SIDE OF THE ANGELS

The basketball team at Texas' John Tarleton College was duly upset when they lost a December 1933 game to San Angelo Junior College. The score was 27–26, and the one-point loss fired up the Tarleton five.

They went on a tear, winning their next 86 games over the next five seasons. But all good things—including winning streaks—come to an end. On February 2, 1938, Tarleton lost again. The winners: San Angelo Junior College. The score? That's right: 27–26!

QUICK REVENGE

On January 24, 1906, East Boston (Mass.) High School murdered Chelsea High, 149–1. On February 8, 1906, just 15 days later, Chelsea turned right around and beat East Boston, 12–11.

There were, of course, explanations for this incredible turnabout. East Boston's Bill Crowley, who scored 95 points in 28 minutes of the first contest, missed the rematch due to illness. And Chelsea had replaced two of its starters.

Perhaps more significantly, however, the second game was played *without backboards*! Only a clean shot could go through the hoop.

SCORER'S DAY OFF

Basketball has come a long way in the last three decades. It had to—after what St. Michael's and Smith, two Massachusetts prep schools, did to it in 1952.

The final score indicated a torrid defensive battle. But perhaps the better word was horrid. When St. Michael's John Sullivan hit a lay-up in the fourth quarter, it marked the game's first points—on the game's first shot!

By the time the buzzer sounded, St. Michael's had gotten off one more shot and Smith had tried four. But Sullivan's bucket held up, and St. Michael's took the 2–0 victory.

PERFECT DAY

The operators of Madison Square Garden must have been pressed for time one day in 1904. They asked Flushing High School (Queens, N.Y.) to play five tournament games in one day.

No trouble! Flushing won 'em all!

EVEN STEVEN

The Big Eight Conference may be better known for football, but its members play some pretty tough basketball, too.

Ample proof is provided by the 1962 game between Colorado and Nebraska. Each team scored 10 field goals in the first half and 10 in the second. Each scored 28 points in the second half, grabbed 29 rebounds, committed 17 personal fouls, and each was awarded 25 free throws.

The only thing that kept the game from lasting all night was a difference in foul shooting. Colorado canned 18 of its free throws and the Cornhuskers only 16. The Buffaloes won 58–56.

A HAHN-Y OF A TEAM

From 1938 to 1962, the Polk (Neb.) High School team always included a Hahn. Beginning with Donald in 1938, the Hahn family then contributed Dwayne, Doyle, Delano, Dolan, and Darwin. Darwin's last two teams won—what else?—the state Class *D* title.

AT LOSE ENDS

The winner of the game between Mars Hill (Miss.) and Enterprise High Schools faced the unhappy prospect of meeting the tournament's top-ranked team.

With this in mind, both teams did everything possible—to lose. With 40 seconds to go, Mars Hill found themselves ahead 20–18. So they tried to snatch defeat from the jaws of victory by tossing two shots into the Enterprise basket. No less enterprising, Enterprise shot the ball into the Mars Hill hoop.

When the final buzzer sounded, Enterprise was a 24–22 winner. But tournament officials had the last word. They bounced *both* teams from the tournament.

LONG DISTANCE BALL

Until the 1940s, basketball was played by relatively normal-sized players. A player who stood 6-1, tiny by today's standards, could play center in those days.

The giants, like 7-0 Bob Kurland of Oklahoma A&M, 6-10 George Mikan of DePaul, and 6-11½ Don Otten of Bowling Green, began to take over in the '40s.

But the little man was far from dead.

On March 14, 1946, a standing-room-only crowd filled New York's Madison Square Garden. The first game of the doubleheader matched Otten's Bowling Green team against Rhode Island. Bowling Green, with its great size, was heavily favored.

The Rhodies, however, didn't give up. They played Bowling Green tough all the way. The game was tied 14 times. But with only three seconds to play, Bowling Green led 74–72.

Rhode Island took the ball out of bounds at midcourt. Bowling Green guarded them closely. Suddenly little 5-10, 140-pound Ernie Calverley broke free. He raced into the clear and received the inbounds pass. No one was guarding him. Unfortunately, he was 55 feet from the basket.

He quickly turned and lofted a high-arching two-handed shot. It seemed to hang in the air for minutes. As everyone in the arena gasped, the shot swished through the hoop, barely disturbing the net. The buzzer sounded. The score was tied 74–74.

Fired up by Calverley's amazing shot, Rhode Island went on to win in overtime.

BUT DID THEY PLAY 4½ INNINGS?

Rainouts are common in baseball. But a rainout in basketball? That's happened, too.

When St. John's (N.Y.) visited Rhode Island on February 3, 1970, the Rams' Keaney Gym was rocking under a vicious ice storm with gale-force winds. And yet every seat was filled. Many more fans were watching on TV all over the east coast.

69

Midway in the game, the officials spotted a wet spot on the floor. "Must be sweat," said one of the men in the striped shirts. He grabbed a towel and mopped it up. But a minute later the puddle was back. The official looked up—and got an eyeful of rain from the roof.

The ice and cold had combined to open one of the hatches on the roof. The maintenance crew was asked to close it. Despite the wind and cold, an aide was dispatched to the roof. But his efforts failed. The water kept pouring in. The officials had no choice. They had to call the game because of "rain."

The teams got together again the following morning. The TV crews were gone; there were no fans in the building. But St. John's went on to win 85–67 in the first rain-delayed game in college basketball history.

MILLER TIME

Forgive the Norte Vista (Cal.) H.S. girls' basketball team if they try to forget the name Cheryl Miller. Cheryl, the 6-2 superstar of Riverside (Cal.) Poly H.S., was the first athlete of *either* sex in *any* sport to make the Adidas All-American High School Team *four times*!

Cheryl had her biggest night ever on January 26, 1982. It was unbeaten Riverside against winless Norte Vista. By the time the dust cleared, Cheryl has tossed in 105 points and Riverside had a 179–15 victory.

Miller was amazing. She hit on 46 of 50 field goal tries and 13 of 15 from the foul line. Her four missed shots included two dunk attempts and two other shots that she tapped in on a second try.

Was Cheryl the first girl to break the 100-point mark? No way. In fact, she was the 15th. And her 105 points weren't even close to the all-time record. That still belongs to Marion Boyd of Maryland's Lonaconing Central H.S., with 156.

ONLY THE LONELY

For four minutes in 1937, Pat McGee of St. Peter's High School (Fairmont, W. Va.) starred in basketball's version of Superman.

Pat and his team of St. Peter's seniors were matched against the school's sophomore team. With four minutes to go, Pat was all alone. All of his teammates had fouled out.

The score was tied, 32–32, and the sophs had a 5-on-1 advantage. But they hadn't counted on McGee's toughness. In the remaining minutes, Pat scored a field goal, canned a free throw—and held the opponents scoreless.

His one-man feat gave his team an incredible 35–32 victory.

ALL OVER
THE FIELD

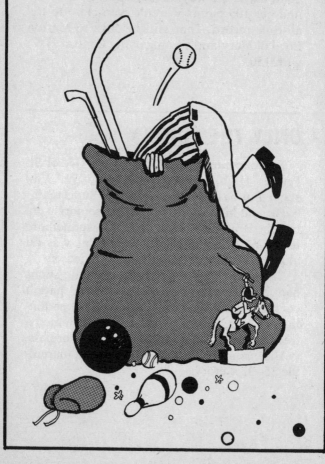

ENDLESS NIGHT

When 5,000 fans settled into their seats for the International Softball Congress world tournament at Saginaw, Mich., on August 18, 1981, they figured they'd be home in a few hours. But the players had other ideas.

The two teams on the field for the 6 P.M. game represented Madison, Wis., and Midland, Mich. Things started routinely. Madison scored a run in the third inning to take a 1–0 lead. Then Midland tied it with a run in the fourth.

The two pitchers, Peter Finn and Peter Meredith, settled down to a good old-fashioned pitching duel. For 29 more innings, neither allowed a run. Then, in the 34th inning, Midland managed to push across the winning run.

Both pitchers, Finn and Meredith, were still on the mound when the marathon ended at 1:23 A.M. Finn struck out 64 opponents, an all-time record, while allowing only nine hits and retiring 36 straight batters at one point. Meredith allowed only 11 hits and struck out 42 batters.

And how many of the original 5,000 fans were still on hand after the 7½-hour contest? Believe it or not, around 3,000. Why? Because there were still three more games on the schedule for that night. Las Vegas, Nev., defeated Charleston, W. Va., 5–1 in a game that ended at 3:37 A.M. Then St. Paul, Minn., beat Oceanside, Cal., 3–1, in a game that finished at 5:41 A.M. And finally, Tulsa, Okla., upended Seattle, Wash., 4–0, in a game that concluded at 7:50 A.M.

A good thing it was, too, because the games scheduled for August 19 were slated to begin at 8 A.M.!

FAR, FAR AWAY

When Senacas Coin's jockey, Jimmy Duff, got to the paddock following the 1949 Kentucky Derby, his first question was, "Who won?" Good question. There's no way that Jimmy could have known the answer.

Senacas Coin was a full quarter of a mile behind the winner, Ponder, when Jimmy pulled the horse out of the race.

That's the way things usually went for Senacas Coin. He started 53 times during his career—and lost 52 times!

THE 12:45 TO CALGARY

Marathon runners are accustomed to all sorts of hazards. They are often bothered by potholes, dogs, even nutty spectators. But freight trains? You can believe it.

Frank Richardson was leading a 1980 marathon in Winnipeg, Canada, when he was forced to make an unscheduled stop. A passing freight train was moving across the marathon course. Richardson figures he lost a full minute waiting for the train to pass. Still, his time of 2:15:15 was outstanding.

The problem was caused, as usual, by human failure. The race official assigned to inform the railroad of the marathon route blew it.

BARGAIN BILL

The Pittsburgh Hard Hats of the American professional Slo-Pitch Softball League had a super week—all in one day. They played a week's worth of games and won 'em all.

The Hard Hats were visiting the New England Pilgrims, and a couple of triple-headers were on tap. But after the first game of the first triple bill, the rains came.

Since the series was scheduled for only two days, the teams decided to tack the two rained-out games onto the next day's scheduled triple-header.

The result: a quintuple-header—five games for the price of one. And Pittsburgh won all five: 7–0, 13–6, 11–4, 11–4, and 11–3.

Even more amazing, the winning pitcher in each game was John Paul.

FISHY STORY

When a racehorse is scratched from a race, there's usually a good reason. The horse may be sick or lame.

But in 1980, when the favorite in a race at South Africa's Milnerton track was scratched, the reason was different.

Quatrain, a prize three-year-old filly, was preparing for her next race when trainer Chris Snaith decided to give her a day off.

"Quatrain needed some rest and relaxation," the trainer remembers. "So I took her to the beach. But while she was wading in the surf, a shark bit her leg."

The shark bite kept Quatrain off the track for a while.

ANOTHER FISHY STORY

Did you ever wish you could play golf and go fishing at the same time? Golfer Graham Whitfield found a way.

Playing at the Oceanside Coomera course in Brisbane, Australia, in October 1976, Whitfield shanked his shot off the eighth tee. The ball headed for a lake, just off the fairway. A fish, swimming in the lake, brought its head out of the water just in time to be conked by Whitfield's off-target shot.

Whitfield, an avid fisherman when he's not playing golf, pulled the two-pound, 14-inch fish out of the water and gave it to a friend.

TOWEL OF STRENGTH

It wasn't pretty, but Lupe Guerra didn't mind. The heavyweight boxer was battling Larry Travis in the first round of a semifinal match in the Omaha (Neb.) Golden Gloves tournament. Suddenly, as Guerra backed away, he heard an all-too-familiar sound. He didn't have to look to know that his boxing trunks had split completely up the back side.

During a quick, emergency time-out, Guerra's trainer grabbed a towel and attached it around the boxer's waist to cover his new "air-conditioned" look. The damage repaired, Guerra went on to a unanimous decision over Travis.

ONCE IN A LIFETIME

The Kentucky Derby may be the world's most famous horse race. Most of the best three-year-old horses make the trip to Louisville, Kentucky, every May for a chance to win the big prize. The winner generally is considered the best three-year-old.

Not so in 1933. It shocked everyone when the race was won by a horse named Brokers Tip. The surprise? He'd never won a race before. Now are you ready for a bigger surprise? He never won another race!

NET WORTH

In sports, this is the age of the specialists. Baseball managers have one lineup against right-handed pitchers, another lineup against lefties. Pro football players are offensive left tackles or strong safeties. Basketball teams have dribblers who always handle the ball late in a close game.

The same is true in soccer. Each of the playing positions is clearly defined. That's why it's most surprising that the winning goalkeeper in the San Jose Earthquakes' 4–3 overtime win over Calgary in 1981 was a sweeper back.

The sweeper back was Tony Powell, a 6-1, 180-pound veteran defensive player. The teams were tied at 3–3, early in overtime. A crossing pass was made in front of the San Jose goal. Goalkeeper Mike Hewitt dived and punched the ball out of the way—and broke his left thumb when he fell.

That's the scene. Now let Tony Powell tell the story:

"I knew right away that Mike was hurt. I yelled to the coach [Jimmy Gabriel] to put in our other goalkeeper. But I forget that we had already used the three substitutes we were permitted to use.

"All the players got together. Before I thought about it, I blurted out: 'Well, I'll go in goal.' I figured that since I was 6-1, I could handle it. And the coach said, 'All right.' And that was it. I was a goalkeeper.

"The fans were making plenty of noise. I switched shirts with the goalkeeper. [Goalkeepers wear a different color than their teammates.] And the show was on. I wasn't too worried. I don't think anyone expected much of me. So there wasn't much pressure. I was the last resort."

Tony did everything a goalie is asked to do. He made two saves, one of which was quite difficult, made the usual number of goal kicks, and passed the ball out when it was necessary.

Eleven minutes later, it all paid off. San Jose's George Best won the game for the 'Quakes with a spectacular goal.

The sweeper back was the winning goalkeeper.

THE LONGEST MILE

The mile run is the glamour event of most track meets. Ever since Roger Bannister broke the fabled four-minute barrier in 1954, runners from every part of the globe have labored long and hard to chip tenths and hundredths of seconds off the world record. The 3:45 mile, once reserved strictly for dreamers, may be just around the corner.

But track fans still like to talk about the longest mile. It happened in February 1950, at the Millrose Games at Madison Square Garden in New York. The Wanamaker Mile, the top event on the program, matched two of America's best milers, Don Gehrmann and Fred Wilt.

As they rounded the final turn, they were neck-and-neck. And when they crossed the finish line, the human eye couldn't separate them. Remember, these were the days before the photo-finish camera.

There were two judges assigned to pick the winner. They both named Fred Wilt. There were two other judges assigned to pick the second-place finisher. *They* both named Fred Wilt. That was impossible, of course, and the judges all argued loud and long. Then they decided to ask the chief judge, Asa Bushnell, to make the pick. He voted for Gehrmann. The winning time: 4 minutes, 9 and $\frac{3}{10}$ seconds.

That was the decision—until a sportswriter named Jesse Abramson protested. Abramson, the track expert for the *New York Herald-Tribune*, stated that the decision was illegal. "The chief judge," he said, "has no right to cast the deciding vote." Abramson suggested that the decision of the first-place judges should stand and that Wilt should be the winner.

Like E. F. Hutton, when Jesse Abramson spoke, everyone listened. The meet directors took their problem to the local Amateur Athletic Union. They, in turn, relayed it to the national AAU. Finally, in December 1950, it was ruled that Fred Wilt was the winner of the Wanamaker Mile.

How long did it take Fred Wilt to win the race? Exactly 10 months, 4 minutes, 9 and $\frac{3}{10}$ seconds!

AND A PARTRIDGE IN A PEAR TREE

When a player is traded, his team usually receives another player or cash or maybe a future draft choice or two. That way, the experts can say, "It's a trade that helps both teams."

But how about the case of Giuseppe Murgia? He was a midfielder for Polisportiva in the Italian Soccer League. When the team decided to get rid of him, they dealt him to the Seulese team. And what did Polisportiva get in return? Would you believe a goat and a piece of prosciutto ham?

It's true. Actually, the two Italian teams were protesting the high fees paid for trades in their league. But probably, as the experts said, "It was a trade that helped *neither* team."

THE WIN THAT WASN'T

For welterweight boxer Johnny Cooper, the victory party was just a case of too much too soon. His four-round victory on November 10, 1981, turned out to be a 10-round defeat.

Late in the fourth round of his fight with Michael Picciotti at Atlantic City, N.J., Cooper had opened a cut above his rival's right eye. Referee Joe O'Neill stopped the fight and asked ring doctor Michael Sabia to check it out. The doctor recommended that the fight be stopped.

O'Neill agreed and awarded the win to Cooper. Johnny and his crew returned to the dressing room and the celebration was on.

It should have waited. New Jersey boxing commissioner, "Jersey Joe" Walcott, a former world heavyweight champion, overturned O'Neill's ruling. "He never checked with the chief doctor," said Walcott. "So I ordered the fight resumed."

Cooper had to return to the ring, where his

hands were retaped and the gloves put back on. With the extended time-out, Picciotti had a chance to recover. He knocked Cooper down in the seventh round and chased him all over the ring in the eighth, ninth, and tenth.

Despite the early pounding, Picciotti piled up enough points in the late going to win a split decision. Then it was his turn to celebrate.

SHOE GOOFS

Willie Shoemaker is one of America's greatest jockeys. And one of its most intelligent!

But it was the Shoe who goofed on Gallant Man, costing his mount the 1957 Kentucky Derby. And it was the same Willie Shoemaker whose misjudgment lost another $100,000 race—the 1956 California Stakes at Hollywood Park.

Shoemaker and the great Swaps zoomed into the stretch, two lengths ahead of second-place Porterhouse. Victory seemed assured.

An eighth of a mile from home, Shoemaker, for some unknown reason, pulled his horse up. He felt Swaps could coast in.

Porterhouse quickly began to make up ground. Shoemaker glanced over his shoulder, spotted Porterhouse, and began pushing Swaps.

Too late. When they swept across the finish line, Porterhouse was a nose in front. The great Willie Shoemaker had blown the race.

DO AS I SAY ...

"I went to the fights the other night," says a comedian, "and a hockey game broke out." Funny, sure. But more than one National Hockey League fan has been turned off by the brawling on the ice.

New York Rangers defenseman Barry Beck decided to do something about it. He wrote an article, under his own by-line, for *The New York Times*. In it, he made a superb case for ending the fighting in the NHL.

A non-fan read it—and loved it. "I've got to see this guy play for myself," he said. And the next time the Rangers suited up, the fan was in the audience. Only he didn't get to see his favorite author. The day the article appeared, Beck began serving a three-game suspension for—what else?—fighting!

UPS AND DOWNS

Boxer Christy Williams would have been better off on a trampoline than in a boxing ring. When he met Battling Nelson on December 26, 1902, Williams hit the floor no fewer than 42 times! That's a careerful of knockdowns, but they all came during one 17-round fight.

Nelson wasn't perfect, either. Williams floored him seven times!

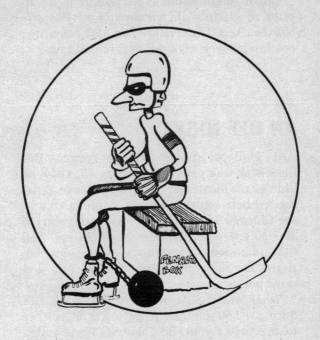

ARREST THAT MAN

Montreal's Chris Nilan is one of the toughest customers in the National Hockey League. At 6-0 and 200 pounds, rival players aren't anxious to do battle with him.

That comes as no surprise to the fans of the Nova Scotia Voyageurs of the American Hockey League. Playing in only 49 games for the Montreal farm club in 1979, Nilan still racked up a league-leading 307 minutes in penalties. That's almost $6\frac{1}{3}$ minutes per game.

But it might come as something of a surprise to Nilan's old classmates at Boston's Northeastern University. The AHL's number one lawbreaker majored in criminal law.

AN OFF NIGHT

If Hall of Fame hockey referee Bill Chadwick was paid on February 20, 1944, he didn't earn his money. Chadwick was working a game between the Toronto Maple Leafs and the Chicago Black Hawks. The game started at 8:30 P.M. and was over by 10:25 P.M. And that included 15-minute intermissions between the first and second and second and third periods.

What was the rush? There was none. But during the 60 minutes of playing time, neither team scored a goal and Chadwick never called a single penalty.

A rarity in the rough-and-tumble world of hockey? You bet. It had never happened before and hasn't again.

LEGEND IN HIS OWN MIND

When Canada won the 1982 World Cup Junior Soccer Tournament in Sydney, Australia, Victor Notaro of Welland, Canada, was a hero. According to Canadian newspapers, 19-year-old Victor scored two goals and assisted on another as Canada defeated West Germany, Brazil, and the Soviet Union to capture the title. In fact, he scored the only goal of the championship game—in the second overtime period.

That was great news. Except that it never happened. The tournament, the play-by-play reports, and the newspaper coverage were all Victor Notaro's idea. He thought it would be a dynamite way for him to clinch Welland's sportsman-of-the-year award.

Each day, he would call his parents "from Australia" with the game results. But Victor was actually attending college at Western Michigan University in Kalamazoo, Mich. His parents relayed the information to the local newspaper, *The Welland Tribune*. Unfortunately, the Welland paper then relayed the news to newspapers throughout Canada and some sports editors became suspicious—but not until after they'd covered the story in full.

When Victor returned home to receive his award, his parents and the local sports editor confronted him with their suspicions. Victor readily admitted that the tournament stories were a hoax. "It was all a fabrication," said his lawyer. "He never really understood that the story would go beyond our town."

Victor went back to Western Michigan, hoping that everyone would forget about it. But for a few days, at least, he had been a national hero.

AT LEAST HE DIDN'T DROWN

How would you like to enter a world competition—when you've never even seen the event before?

That's what happened to two runners from Guinea-Bissau (which used to be Portuguese Guinea) during the 1979 Spartakiad Games in Moscow. The two, Bernardo Vilela and U Sejidi, were scheduled to compete in the 3,000-meter steeplechase. In this nearly two-mile race, the runners are asked to jump over hurdles placed all around the track. But when the race began, it became clear that neither one had ever seen a hurdle before.

Vilela ran first. Each time he came to a barrier, he stopped and jumped over the hurdle with both feet. (Hurdlers normally lead with one foot, then bring the other foot over.) When he heard the bell, which signals that there is one lap to go, he stopped again. "Is the race over?" he asked. "No," answered the meet officials. "Keep running."

With the crowd cheering him along, he raced on. At one of the last hurdles, he leaped up onto the hurdle, then fell backward.

In the next race, U Sejidi became the center of attraction. When he got to the first hurdle, he tripped and landed flat on his face. He picked himself up and ran on. At the next two hurdles, he grabbed the barrier and lifted himself over.

Then he got to the water jump. This is a hurdle standing in front of a 12-foot long, shallow pool of water. He was already way behind the other runners. He stopped, looked at the hurdle and the water, shook his head, and walked quickly off the track.